THIS NOTEBOOK BELONGS TO

2

Author & Publisher: Lars Edingloh, Neuer Graben 49, 44139 Dortmund, Germany
Print: Amazon Media EU S.à r.l., 5 Rue Plaetis, L-2338, Luxembourg

Made in the USA
Monee, IL
05 June 2025

18793379R10073